INDEPENDENT KIRKUS

An unconventional, strategic approach to optimizing business profits.

Bielat and Bryan (The BestPossible Enterprise, 2013) are champions of "Enterprise Optimization," or "EO," a method that Bryan created that's intended to help drive companies "towards new levels of profitability." Their book is, in essence, a concise, well-written description of EO's conceptual design as well as a discussion of its benefits. The challenge, however, is that EO is not widely known and is somewhat unconventional. It relies on computer models to test "all of the possibilities within the realities of your company's complexities" and help leaders make the best use of what the authors characterize as five basic resources: capital, procurement options, sales opportunities, production capabilities, and information. (The titular "Profit Hawks," they explain, are business leaders who employ EO to "make the best use of their limited resources in pursuit of optimal profits.") Not surprisingly, the authors believe that strategic planning is more critical to success than tactical or operational planning, asserting that it "typically offers the greatest bottom-line, advantage, yet is the least common in companies that are locked into defensive, cost-based management." This, in fact, is the central argument of the book: that companies must radically change their decision-making processes if they are to achieve "best-possible" performance and profitability. This book does an admirable job of explaining the EO methodology completely yet succinctly as well as justifying its use. Still, the book concentrates almost entirely on the high-level benefits of EO while neglecting the specifics of how to implement it. Several question-and-answer sections bring the discussion down to a functional level, but it might have been helpful to cite a few concrete, real-life examples to provide evidence of EO's validity to reassure business leaders.

Some readers may find this a forward-thinking overview of an intriguing profit-oriented methodology, but others are likely to be more skeptical of its practical applications. – *Kirkus Reviews*

Bielat/Bryan: We are proud of the review, even the criticism, and chose to share it in its entirety. Our intent was to make this a quick, impactful read for the busy leaders that will make the most of *Profit Hawks*. Our goal is not to sell books, it is to spread the opportunity of Enterprise optimization. We measure our success by how many leaders achieve new levels of profit. We hope you are one of them.

STEEL DYNAMICS STRUCTURAL + Rail mill
is a profit Hawk case study

PROFIT HAWKS

CAPTURE THE PROFITS BEING LOST EVERY
DAY TO THE COMPLEXITY OF YOUR BUSINESS

Andrew C. Bielat
Eugene L. Bryan, Ph.D.

Copyright © 2016 Andrew C. Bielat and Eugene L. Bryan

All rights reserved.

No part of this may be reproduced in any form or in any means, electronic or mechanical, including photocopying, scanning, recording by any information storage or retrieval system, without the permission in writing from the publisher. (If interested, please send your request to info@profithawk.com.)

BestPossible® trademark is registered by Eugene L. Bryan.

ISBN 10: 0692602828

ISBN 13: 9780692602829

Library of Congress Control Number

Printed in the United States of America.

Order at www.amazon.com

Contents

Chapter 1

Introduction

Please try something before you continue reading the rest of this book. Take a quick break from the details of your everyday responsibilities and thoughts. Think instead for a minute about making a bet, a big one, then add more to it—a huge bet. Imagine the bet is on you and your ability break through to a whole new level of profit. Think about betting your personal future on that growth, and that growth alone. What target are you imagining? How do you feel about the bet?

You're reading this book because you want your company to be really good, exceptional, great, thought of highly by your peers, the market, and your associates. You've already achieved a certain level of success, and you're looking for the next level. You've proven that you have done a lot of things right and continue to do so, but you also know that reaching the upper echelon of performance isn't achieved easily and that it's going to take more than repeating your past performance. Becoming the best is a process of innovation and leadership on the offensive, not brute force and defense of the past.

In his book *Good to Great*, James Collins wrote, "good is the enemy of great," meaning that so many leaders are satisfied with good that they never pursue, or even envision, greatness. What did greatness look like to you in your imagination?

If you could only win the imaginary bet by making profit gains that would be clearly defined as great, both in the short term and throughout the remainder of your career, what would you need to succeed?

What if we told you that by reading this book and applying its principles, you would have everything you need to achieve your best-possible performance, greatness?

We are telling you that, and you can. The reality is that you are most likely already doing as much, or more, work as is necessary to make your business the best it can possibly be. It won't take more work, it will take the right tools and practices. The right tools for the job, used in the right way. Each and every time, over several decades, the concepts of Enterprise Optimization (EO) described in this book have been applied the companies have produced sustainable and dramatic growth.

The tools and concepts are not part of a flavor-of-the-month management initiative that will get displaced by the next leadership innovation. They are not theoretical, but instead are based on real world, practical application, well established technology and, most importantly, they work for any leader willing to make the transition.

If you're like most seasoned leaders you probably experience one or more of five common frustrations:

1. Profit: Simply put, there's not enough of it.
2. The ceiling: You've got good people working hard and committed to the business, but you can't break through to the next level doing it the way you're doing it.
3. Nothing's working: You've tried various strategies and quick fixes. None have worked in the long run and your staff is numb to new initiatives.
4. Defensiveness: After putting in all the effort to conceive and try new things, the team, and you, are on the defensive. There seem to be more reasons to NOT try things than exciting new ideas.
5. Insecurity: Unsure of how good they could or should be doing, people withdraw into silos, keeping their heads down, creating doubt, which slowly permeates the organization.

Granted, a small minority of business leaders and owners do not suffer these frustrations. They run their business with everyone focused on the prize, working together for their best-possible performance. The leaders and staffs are more in control, happier, more creative and spend most of their time on the offense, having fun doing what they know they are great at. They even have more profit to work with. Most of us, though, aren't there yet.

This book contains the concepts and describes the tools you need to enable your company to get there; to achieve its best-possible performance. Although you can't do it alone as the leader of an organization, it does require you, and you alone, to make the decision to become a great company. Not a good company, not a company that is better than the competition, not a company that is better than it was last year, a truly great company. We will describe the decision later as one where you simply choose to be a "BestPossible®" company.

These concepts and tools didn't come to us over night; in fact they have been refined and improved over the last 50 years through countless hands-on real-world experiences, one lesson at a time. It started as a quest by my mentor and partner, Eugene "Gene" L. Bryan, Ph.D., to optimize profits of a plywood mill using computer technology in the 1960s. It worked. It was an unqualified success, adding, in today's dollars, more than $9 million in profits over the first year. That was where Enterprise Optimization started and today it is more powerful and accessible than ever.

Over the years, with well over 500 applications, Gene's hands-on coaching, problem solving, research, and writing has refined the practices of helping companies become the best they can be. He is considered by many as the Founding Father of Enterprise Optimization. I am blessed to have connected with him and even more so, for his decision to act as my mentor and become a partner on our mission.

Independent of Gene's work, as a frustrated corporate executive in the 1990s, I drew from my engineering background and built my own LP optimization model at a large steel plant. That first-time, inexperienced effort worked to add $120 thousand per month to our bottom line. Since starting my own consulting and software services firms, I have worked with 76 companies, coaching over 60 senior executive leaders, providing leadership workshops to more than 1,500 managers and supervisors, and applied the Profit Hawk tools and concepts to produce hundreds of millions of dollars in profit growth.

The last several years have been a whirlwind of exciting progress. Incorporating Gene's knowledge, experience, and wisdom into our efforts has resulted in "Profit Hawk" as we know it today, an optimization-based leadership system, a vital leadership role in enterprise optimization, our first book, *The BestPossible Enterprise*, and now this book.

At this moment, people who follow the Profit Hawk principles are realizing improved teamwork, increased energy and focus, enhanced self-confidence, more profits, and more fun. Our clients typically increase their profits by at least three percent of their revenue the first year and then continue like gains year after year.

EO isn't a one-time breakthrough. You will find that the ability to make best-possible decisions increases confidence and team effectiveness from day-one. You will start identifying goals and breaking through constraints that weren't even in the picture prior to becoming Profit Hawks. And best of all, you will start making your BestPossible better, for as long as you run your enterprise.

Consider a sailboat race from Los Angeles to Hawaii. Whom would you bet on to win the race if one team is using GPS to navigate and the other team is using maps, charts, and a sextant?

It is obvious who will win—and why. One team knows the best course and the right adjustments continuously throughout the race. The other teams are repeatedly missing opportunities hidden from them by their technology—and they don't even know that they missed them.

Just as the captain with the GPS doesn't have to learn a new language of sailing and leadership, you don't have to learn an endless stream of new words or techniques to capture more profits. Instead, you will replace burdensome, complex, and often conflicting processes with clarity, objectivity, and confidence. Join us on this journey to your BestPossible.

As you and your team learn to fully employ the practices you will make quicker decisions, grow more rapidly as leaders, keep your people more engaged on the right things, and focus more effectively on your ever-improving vision.

We have a tremendous amount of respect for every leader out there, from the lead-man on the floor to the CEO of the enterprise. You hold the future of your associates, owners, suppliers, customers, and communities in your hands. You take risks and you make big decisions. You build visions and help others fulfill their dreams. Our passion and mission is to help you succeed and we hope this book will help you start and stay on the journey to your BestPossible.

Q *We are already doing better than most of our competitors. We must be doing something right. Can Enterprise Optimization technology help, given how well we are already doing?*

A The question to ask yourself isn't, "How good are we today?" It is, "How good could you be today?"

As a successful company, you are probably doing most things right, and so are your competitors. To be the BestPossible, we need to do the right things in the right amounts at the right times in the right ways. You can certainly survive and even prosper doing things better than most of your competitors, and for many, that is good enough.

However, if you want your company to excel, you have to know how good you can be, which is not identifiable with spreadsheet models and traditional cost-based management.

Once even the best-performing teams clearly see that there are substantial opportunities to grow, they are routinely able to generate profit growth greater than 3 percent of revenue. The better the team, the greater the gains when they know what they could be achieving.

Chapter *2*

Hidden Profits

This might be the hardest pill to swallow as leaders. No matter how smart or talented we are—you, your team, your boss, your Board of Directors, everyone included—we aren't smart enough to put all of our options and constraints together and simultaneously solve for the optimal profits.

The critical question we have to ask ourselves is, "How do we know that what we are doing today isn't leaving profits on the table?" If that hasn't got you thinking hard enough, ask yourself, "How many times have I seen things we missed that cost us profits during a given period of time?"

And the clincher, "How much do we miss and never realize what we could have had?"

Business has been done, and decisions have been made in much the same ways for the last several generations of leadership. Many have prospered but, too often, continue to cling to what they have done in the past because "it worked." This book is written for those ready to take the next step toward new levels of profitability—Enterprise Optimization.

What you do with this information will define you and, maybe more importantly, define the future performance of your business.

We have done our best to keep the book concise and actionable by including the right amount of detail for you to fully consider taking advantage of the concepts, the "what," without getting sidetracked by the implementation necessities, the "how." We know from experience that once you make the decision to pursue these concepts, as a leader or a Profit Hawk, all else will follow, and follow more naturally than you might expect.

All companies have never-ending, profit-sensitive decisions to make where the complexities of trade-offs and ripple effects obscure opportunities to earn additional bottom-line profits.

The key to capitalizing on Enterprise Optimization (EO) is recognizing and accepting that:

- The decisions you and your team make directly and inevitably determine your level of success.
- All companies have never-ending, profit-sensitive decisions to make.
- Complexities of trade-offs and ripple effects obscure opportunities to earn additional bottom-line profits.

Accept these, and you can take control of your future; it's all about decision-making.

Decisions being made in the "gray" or "wrong" are costing profits—untold amounts are lost forever.

Every decision has an objective in mind, and how well it serves its objective is the measure of the decision's effectiveness. *Wrong* means the decision could not have been worse—it was dead wrong. Similarly, *right* means it could not have been better—it was the best-possible choice for our objective given our circumstances. In between are gray-area decisions that will yield mixed results—some favorable, some not, some much more productive than others.

Consider a continuum of decision quality (see Figure 2.1). The more complex a company's decision environment, the greater the distance between the ends of its decision continuums and the more its shades of gray become a fog. In fog, it's hard to tell which direction we're moving—if we're moving at all.

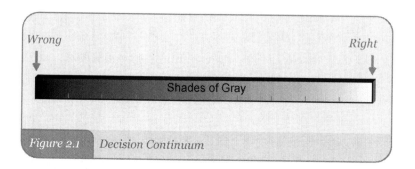

Figure 2.1   *Decision Continuum*

When the decisions being made are in the "gray" or "wrong," they are costing profits—untold amounts are lost forever.

Contrary to past practices, sustained success today requires more than matching wits, costs, and production numbers with those of competitors. It requires leading-edge methods and technologies to manage our complexities as effectively as possible.

Consistently exceptional performance is never the result of chance; it requires a well-defined destination and the determination to get there. You have to know what the best you can achieve is to have any realistic chance of getting there.

The Situation

Application of the concepts and technologies described in this book have, without fail, produced gains that have always been large. Initial gains have typically ranged from $30,000 to $70,000 in added profits for every million dollars in sales.

So how can it be that these gains are available to even healthy, successful companies?

Remember the Rubik's Cube? Dr. Erno Rubik of the Budapest School of Applied Arts created his simple-looking puzzle with only two basic variables: color and position. But his calculations showed that its six colors and fifty-four positions have 43,252,003,274,489,856,000 (43 billion-billion) possible patterns. You can see why it is not possible to solve his puzzle without a system (an algorithm, a solution) to adjust and control the position of its individual elements while working toward its optimal solution of six uniformly colored sides.

Virtually all companies are more complex than Rubik's Cube. Every company has more complexity in the number, and interactions, of controllable and noncontrollable variables. With near-infinite possible patterns of procurement, production, and sales activities, the performance of companies within most industries varies widely. We find operations on the brink of bankruptcy as others enjoy great returns. This range of performance is largely related to complexity—the more variables there are to manage, the greater an industry's range of bottom-line results.

Traditionally, companies have handled complexity through simplification—they departmentalize improvement activities, intentionally or unintentionally, effectively reducing the numbers and complexities of each department's decisions, depending on the leaders to "know their numbers." This causes profit-draining conflicts as individuals work to optimize their department's face of "the cube" while inadvertently and inevitably messing up those of other departments. Optimal performance calls for integrated decision-making and teamwork to ensure best-possible bottom-line results.

Given Rubik's 43 billion-billion possible patterns, it should be clear that companies of all kinds and sizes have plenty of immediate profit gains hidden in the complexities of their business, whatever their circumstances. This is more a reality of human limitations than an issue of leadership competence. We refer to the hidden profit opportunities as profit gaps, and profit gaps are facts of life. The good news: your company's profit gap is also your *field of opportunities* (see Figure 2.2).

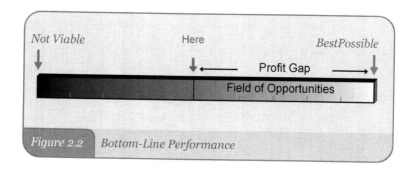

Figure 2.2   *Bottom-Line Performance*

The Solution

The solution to uncovering your true profit potential, and capturing those profits as a team, are specialized tools that can lead you to your best-possible level of performance; the traditional decision-making tools cannot get you there.

The solution, true optimization systems, use algorithms, and supportive technologies designed to solve the cube-puzzle that is your business, simultaneously testing all of the possibilities within the realities of your company's complexities. The optimization function is not to test ideas but to define best-possible performance and the necessary, integrated plans to achieve it.

Spreadsheets, which have been ubiquitously applied and re-lied upon, can only effectively test self-conceived ideas one at a time among billions of interrelated possibilities. They do not maintain relationships with productivity or include market and other enterprise constraints.

One of your most significant challenges to implementing the solution will be that each member of your leadership team has to step out of the comfort zone of how things have been done and embrace the new tools and practices.

Without the aid of Enterprise Optimization technologies, even the best of corporations are unable to solve their "Rubik's Cube."

Once you decide to pursue optimizing your enterprise, you will find that it is challenging, but it is not particularly difficult. In fact, every good company is already putting more time and energy into traditional performance analysis and improvement efforts than will be necessary with the new, more effective tools and methods. Most importantly, without these improved meth-ods, even the best leaders will continue to fall far short of their full potential—they are literally incapable of solving their Ru-bik's Cube.

We trust you have decided by now to continue through this book since, for most, the decision is an easy one, not gray at all. We know that most progressive leaders will quickly recognize the challenge and have already decided to find a way to solve your cube. Welcome to the realm of the Profit Hawk.

Fundamentals

In order to keep this book concise we need to establish a basic language and conceptual common ground. Please bear with us, it really is necessary and will help you get the most out of your time. There is always more to learn, but that learning should occur while in the process since immediate gains are waiting right now.

As you read, you may, like many, have sensed these truths but have been unable to put the whole picture together for yourself or when trying to influence your team to make the best-possible decisions.

You may at first see the lessons in this book as mostly common sense, which means you are likely a natural Profit Hawk. With a little more thought, you'll realize that even though they are common sense, these lessons are not often recognized or applied systematically.

Profit is not a reason for success; it is a measure of success; and it is an essential source of strength for all enterprises. It is the bottom line.

Here are a few definitions that are important to the discussion of Enterprise Optimization and the role of the Profit Hawk:

- *BestPossible*: As a noun, the highest achievable level of accomplishment, given existing capabilities and circumstances
- *Enterprise*: Any complex undertaking that involves considerable scope and risk and is dependent on others for success
- *Enterprise Optimization* (EO): A systematic process of planning, integrating, coordinating, and executing all dimensions of enterprise activities for optimal profits
- *Profit*: Any gain resulting from successful action (In business this is monetary.)
- *Profit Hawk*: A person who applies EO tools and practices to support decision-making aimed at BestPossible bottom-line performance
- *Optimal profits*: Best-possible profits that can be achieved symbiotically (In business, this means symbiotically across all five types of constituents of an enterprise: owners, employees, customers, suppliers, and communities. Maximum profits are often achieved on the short term and at the expense of the constituents.)

Profit Hawk Concepts

About Profit

It is vital to recognize that profit is not a reason for success; it is a measure of success; and it is an essential source of strength for all enterprises. It is the bottom line. If we spend more than we make, our venture will eventually run out of gas and slow to a stop. When we earn more than we need to sustain our pace, we have the opportunity to accelerate our growth. With more capital, we can acquire more talent, materials, equipment, and technologies for a longer and more rewarding journey.

Profit Hawks are not focused on surviving; they stay on offense applying these concepts and technologies to thrive and win repeatedly on a continuous journey to Destination BestPossible.

All companies can benefit from the role of Profit Hawks…to increase bottom-line profits.

Applicability

These concepts are applicable for all companies within all industries since all enterprises acquire and use resources as they work to create and deliver value to customers. All business owners and leaders face challenges as they work to optimize and integrate their sales, procurement, and production activities. Although many think of their businesses as simple operations, nearly all enterprises have enough complexity to benefit greatly from the EO concepts and tools.

All companies can benefit from the role of Profit Hawks and their ability to identify, quantify, and help capture the best opportunities to increase bottom-line profits.

About Change

We do what we do because our thoughts, analyses, and traditions tell us they are the right things to do. Otherwise, we would not do them. This means all of us have what seem to be good reasons to defend our ways and resist change. This must be understood if you are to embrace and influence change.

Nobody wants his or her past decisions and practices invalidated. But the decision to use a GPS device to win a race to Hawaii does not invalidate the prior reliance on charts and a sextant. If all we had to use in the past were spreadsheets and cost-based management tools, there is no reason for us to apologize for not seeing hidden profit opportunities or knowing our full potential. It does not make us inadequate leaders to have used traditional approaches before becoming aware of better tools and methods.

Excuses

There are no valid, objective excuses for continuing down the same path; the technology exists; and most leaders have a passion for being as good as they can be at what they do. Why not become, or embrace, a Profit Hawk in the pursuit of your company's BestPossible? Give it some thought and see if your reasons are addressed as you read on.

Q *We have obvious things that need fixing; does it make sense to take this initiative on right now?*

A The "full-plate syndrome" often stands in the way of greatness. What can be more important than finding out what you need to be doing to optimize your profits?

Your team is busy working on activities, making commitments for completion, and holding each other accountable for the commitments, but they are ultimately wasting time, energy, and profits if they are working on less-than-optimal activities, without ever knowing it. It's as if they are climbing a mountain and believe they are moving uphill, but the fog is so thick they may be wasting every step as they climb into impassable canyons.

You don't have to let your team struggle without verifying that their efforts will produce optimal results when you have an EO system. Teams often end up choosing to withdraw from major initiatives once they can see through the fog and are invariably able to improve their route.

Chapter 3

Optimization is Optimal

No matter how well you are doing, you could be doing better if you aren't optimizing, by definition, logic, and in practice.

As you read that statement, somewhere deep in the reptilian part of your brain, you might have thought something like, "Well that is not always true..." or, "Maybe not under certain conditions." We can't help ourselves, we are human and take great pride in our intelligence and businesses knowledge, rightfully so.

The most frequent "condition" we encounter where people think EO isn't necessary is when the markets are bad. It's then that we hear, "we have to take whatever comes our way, those decisions are easy."

Does that make sense? Is decision making less important when business is bad? When are you under the most pressure to "lead" the way to better results? Do the decisions really get easy?

All good leaders work on growing their businesses and engaging their employees, and most are diligent about assessing their performances and seeking out improvements. However, leaders are bombarded with cost-based improvement ideas and information that are, at best, partial solutions and not the panaceas that they were hoped to be, including capital projects, ERPs, Lean Manufacturing, and Six Sigma. Some of these are fairly easy to implement while others can be highly disruptive and take years to become fully beneficial, if they ever do. Some are localized opportunities that never produce bottom-line improvements and may even cost the company profits.

EO...it's not a trendy concept; it's simply the best way to engage an entire organization in a common pursuit of the best they can be.

Enterprise Optimization (EO) is different. It's not a trendy concept; it's simply the best way to engage an entire organization in a common pursuit of the best they can be; it is the pursuit of BestPossible.

Profit Hawks, when fully armed with technology and knowledge, offer the best approach to what every business leader is already trying to do: make the best use of their limited resources in pursuit of optimal profits—Enterprise Optimization. The game changer is the ability to provide far better information for making the decisions and commitments that are critical to growth and success. More about them and their capabilities in the next chapter.

You will find that every operation has its own unique performance continuum, field of opportunities, and BestPossible —which is always a viable target. Much like how GPS works for navigating to a specific point, EO systems tell us where we are relative to our optimal-profit target—allowing us, often for the first time, to pinpoint our position under ever-changing circumstances and know what we need to do to get to our destination.

The bottom-line value and competitive advantages to be gained with EO are the results of the ability to do the following:

- Identify and quantify opportunities for improvement
- Provide fully integrated departmental plans
- Quantify accomplishments and chart progress toward BestPossible
- Discover ways to make BestPossible better

Bottom-line gains are in the range of 3 percent to 7 percent of total sales revenue.

Within most industries, fields of opportunities are expansive, leading to initial bottom-line gains in the range of 3 percent to 7 percent of total sales revenue—without additional capital investments.

So why wouldn't everyone immediately jump at the opportunity to apply EO?

The most prominent reason is that the unconventional practices of Enterprise Optimization are not taught explicitly in any university or business school yet. Most leaders do not know that it is available to them.

Even when leaders understand the potential of an EO system, they recognize the cost and investment required to design and develop software in house—which is impractical unless your core business is complementary software. The decision to build and deploy an in-house system has been a predominant reason for failures of EO efforts.

Additionally, when some leaders are first exposed to the practices, we have heard comment such as these:

- "We don't have the time; our plate is full right now."
- "We don't have the data we need."
- "We have spreadsheets that do all that."
- "We aren't even good at the basics yet—come back when we have our act together."
- "Our business is too complicated to model accurately."

These assertions stem from a lack of understanding, complacency, natural defensiveness, or a combination of them all. Anyone truly aware of the potential rewards will reject complacency, stop defending business as usual, and immediately make room on his or her plate. Soon they'll happily find their plates largely cleared by the optimization processes.

Identifying and achieving the best-possible performance is not just another improvement project—it is the obligation [of] every leader.

There can be no better time than now to change the trajectory of your business. What can be more important than defining and moving systematically toward your very own Best-Possible? After all, identifying and achieving the best-possible performance is not just another improvement project—it is the obligation every leader has to their constituency and to themselves.

Intangible Benefits

Rewards
The rewards reach far beyond monetary profits. The emotional rewards of high-level success are what really drive teams. Teams perform best when working toward common, exciting goals. Teamwork and synergy come naturally from the integration and coordination required for high-level performance.

Inspiration
BestPossible is inherently inspirational. Its two parts have deep meaning: *best*—nothing can be better, and *possible*—it can be done, you can get there from wherever you are starting. It recognizes your current mission along with all of your opportunities, limitations, capabilities, and circumstances. When people know they are putting their time and energy into something that can be great, their attitudes and behaviors change—always for the better.

Innovation
People often assume BestPossible implies perfection, an unrealistic standard. In fact, not only is it realistic but we can often do better than today's BestPossible by using creativity to get past our current obstacles that limit it. We can make gains within our

current boundaries, but our greatest opportunities lie beyond to-day's perceptions, constraints, policies, and practices. Tomorrow, we can leave today's BestPossible standing as a mile-post in our rearview mirror.

Applications

Once the Enterprise Optimization system is available, it can be used to improve all profit-sensitive decisions. Every use provides fresh knowledge based on current capabilities, limitations, and opportunities. Ultimately it always seeks the answer to a universal question, "What do we need to do to earn best-possible profits under existing or predicted market conditions?" The applications are nearly unlimited and include the following:

Business Planning Optimization

- Mergers and acquisitions
- Annual forecasting with interim adjustments in response to changing circumstances
- Integrated, enterprise-wide strategies and tactics
- Expansions, curtailments, divestitures, and alliances

Production

- Optimizing use of all production capabilities
- Staffing/crew additions, cutbacks, and uses of overtime hours
- In-context net profitability analysis of production-related capital projects

Sales

- Sales and operations planning (S&OP) to pursue

the sweet spot for profitability: the optimal product/customer/service mix

- Evaluating and pricing new offerings, special orders, and sales contracts
- Strategic product pricing/volume profitability, in-context of trade-offs and ripple effects

Procurement

- Optimizing raw material bidding, buying, inventory, and purchase contracts
- Evaluating make-or-buy opportunities for finished and/or semifinished goods

Q *How would the system help us plan and justify capital improvements?*

A Opportunity values (explained in chapter 10, The Science) from your system will show where capital investments will add the most to your bottom line. You can examine these opportunities more closely by modeling new equipment in your system to see how things change.

EO systems consider the optimum product mix, any and all bottlenecks, cost of downtime, increases and decreases in work activities, and all other big-picture consequences of any change. This process creates a highly reliable justification where you will not only know the bottom-line value of proposed new equipment, but you'll know in advance how to use that equipment to optimally leverage all other assets.

In many cases, the system exposes how spending more and addressing related constraints simultaneously produces a far greater return on the invested capital.

Chapter 4

The Profit Hawk

The primary reason Enterprise Optimization has remained out of the mainstream is that it isn't taught as a discipline in colleges. This leaves the role of the Profit Hawk in an organization a non-traditional hybrid. Many leaders think like Profit Hawks, but no being fully armed with the tools and practices, organizational inertia forces them back into a traditional box, making decisions in traditional ways, getting traditional results.

Possibly the most exciting opportunity for a high-potential performer is to become one of the leadership team's Profit Hawks. The opportunity to expose and capture millions of profit-dollars along with the extraordinary learning are a unique proposition. Can you think of a better growth opportunity?

If a company is to approach its BestPossible performance, its senior leaders have to fully support the Enterprise Optimization processes. A leader halfheartedly applying the concepts, or any business practice for that matter, creates doubts within his or her team and limits progress. Even when the leaders fully support optimization, they can't attain it without a few key personnel—their Profit Hawks.

What It Means

The title "Profit Hawk" is a description of the role the leader in charge of EO plays. The two words have this meaning:

- *Profit*—the natural measure of success. All living things either profit and flourish or they die off. Critically, a company on the road to best-possible intentionally ensures their profits feed the five constituents of their business ecosystem: customers, employees, owners, suppliers, and communities.

- *Hawks*—widely respected and admired, known for their shrewd and exceptional hunting skills, able to pounce on opportunities hidden where others are unable to capitalize on them. When operating effectively, a Profit Hawk is a highly respected member of the leadership team. They are uniquely able to find opportunities that are otherwise hidden by the complexity of their business.

What They Offer

Well-equipped and trained Profit Hawks can put to rest two nagging questions:

- Are the goals and plans we are developing optimal, or even viable?
- Is our performance due to our leadership and execution or to changing market factors?

In the past, without any better way to develop goals, teams traditionally ended up using rhetorical command goals ("we have to achieve better numbers") and strategies based on the creativity and intuition of senior executives ("that's what they get paid for, to make decisions and set goals").

The process nearly always included accounting-based spreadsheet models, subjective analysis of market projections, and a common acceptance that "better" is always good—better than last month, better than last-year-same-period, better than the competition, and so on.

When that was the standard, we could all be comfortable that we were doing the best we could. In fact, most smart and dedicated teams do generate some growth by setting goals this way and pursuing them. There is also a general satisfaction within most teams that if they are pulling together, and the board/owners are happy with the performance, they must be doing the right thing.

With simply what you know now, accepting business as usual is equivalent to leaving significant profits on the table, knowing that you are not optimizing the use of your resources or the creativity of your team.

Without the use of a Profit Hawk's EO practices, there is no dependable way to answer these four key questions:

1. How far are we from the best-possible profits?
2. What are the profit-limiting constraints that we can address?
3. What is the full-context, bottom-line profitability of the improvement initiatives proposed?
4. What is our real performance, excluding market effects?

Not a guess, not a better-than-last goal, not a wishful destination, not just better than the competition, but the actual, here and now, best-possible bottom-line we can achieve.

The Profit Hawk's role becomes, first and foremost, to reliably answer these questions by identifying the best-possible profit potential of your business under the current conditions and with the existing resources and capabilities. Not a guess, not a better-than-last goal, not a wishful destination, not just better than the competition, but the actual, here and now best-possible bottom-line we can achieve.

A second unique responsibility is to engage the entire team. That requires that Profit Hawks learn enough to ensure that every member of their teams believes in the goal, has clear plans to pursue it, and is committed to making it happen. Don't worry if this sounds unrealistic; it is being done right now at many companies; and it is more natural than you might think. The process becomes as fundamental to successful business as the computer itself.

There are many would-be Profit Hawks out there, by nature or by ambition. What better role in your career could you have?

Who They Are

Profit Hawks are by nature one of the most important leaders in any organization. They are ambitious, persistent, intelligent, team-oriented, practical, and comfortable with technology. They become best-possible navigators in support of the visions of their company's senior leaders.

The opportunity for these individuals is unique in the business world. They are able to learn more about the company's end-to-end, procurement-to-customer, full-context, effects on bottom-line profits than in any other role in the company. The most effective hawks lead through objective persuasion, with empathy and an understanding of the challenges the other leaders face. They create solid, respectful relationships and gain exposure to the profit implications of every aspect of the business.

The Profit Hawk role is often mistaken to be simply an accounting or information-technology-specific role. Although any ambitious leadership-oriented individual can be a Profit Hawk, the most natural fits are the next-generation operations and sales leaders with an interest in fact-based leadership and bottom-line performance.

The role is not necessarily a full-time position. By playing complementary leadership roles, Profit Hawks are able to keep their street smarts. Those street smarts enable them to maintain one of the most beneficial traits of a hawk—their ability to cut through the fog of bias, defensiveness, and self-limiting paradigms to clear the path to greater performance.

Finally, because the practices they master are universally applicable, whatever endeavor or opportunity Profit Hawks pursue, they will be prepared to pounce confidently on it, exceeding all expectations, and helping everyone along the way.

Once quantified, the constraints that currently hold your enterprise back are all surmountable.

Profit Hawks have to be open-minded. Some of what they learn and promote is counterintuitive, flying in the face of traditional business mantras and paradigms and, because of that, offering exceptional learning opportunities for everyone involved. The Profit Hawks are able to deal with realities that are not always easy to handle in corporate culture, including these insights:

- The greatest opportunities for any business lie beyond the self-imposed limits that shape its paradigms.
- Once quantified, all constraints that hold your enterprise back are surmountable.
- Enterprise Optimization is more efficient, rewarding, and effective than accounting-based decision-making systems, and importantly, it feeds your creativity.
- BestPossible gets better as we get better and as we gain

resources and skills and as our team becomes more confident, creative, systematic, and enthusiastic—more effective.

If you are considering the role of Profit Hawk, what are your thoughts as you read these bullet points? Are you able to validate each of these statements with what you know right now? What would your boss or peers think if you asserted any of these ideas as facts today?

Don't be concerned if any of these seem foreign to you or might seem unusual to your associates. By the time you finish this book, you will be able to fully explain each of them and enthusiastically pursue your potential.

Q *Our production processes, products, and customers are very complex. I don't see how they can be accurately modeled. How does that work?*

A The fundamental reason for the invention of linear programming (LP) models (explained in chapter 10, The Science) was to overcome our human analytical limitations and empower our creativity.

The more complicated an enterprise, the more opportunity the systems have to analyze the best-possible combination of products and service based on production capabilities, market opportunities, and costs to maximize profits. Because LP models, using activity-based costs, accurately model the physical processes of any operation, if you currently produce it and know how it became an end product, the modeling is simply a matter of identifying the unique process steps required for each product or product type.

Even the simplest preliminary LP model of a complex enterprise will produce superior, directionally correct, decision-making support to increase profits.

Chapter 5

The New Game

The late football coach Vince Lombardi relied on the basics for his team's success; these were blocking (on offense) and tackling (on defense). Most of us tend to see business in much the same way—take on the competition while on offense and try to hold ground on defense. Leaders too often see the game of business as a contest among competitors.

When playing the EO game it is different. The main obstacles standing between your team and the goal line are outdated traditions and restricted visions. Competitors are part of the landscape, but not the focus of attention.

Rather than being a contact sport, EO is an individual competition such as a foot race or a golf match, where those who show up and perform to their potential win without confrontation.

The Rules

The better you know the rules, the better the chance you have to win any game—in this case, the game of Enterprise Optimization, which is trying to achieve your BestPossible bottom-line performance. Some of these rules are familiar; others are new or considered in new ways.

Opportunity-Based Leadership

Winning the game requires offense, and a leader's only offense is in pursuit of opportunities, where all growth occurs. Yet the predominant focus of leaders for generations has been cost-based management, a necessary but mostly defensive approach. These strategies, tactics, and operational initiatives are designed to reduce costs in hopes of increasing the bottom line. Countless hours and other resources have been dedicated to reducing costs with results that often limited success. Once costs are at their optimal levels, any additional reductions will take away profits.

Many of the cost-reduction efforts look good in isolation but ultimately result in losses through unrecognized ripple effects and trade-offs.

Even more detrimental to the organization, cost-based management reduces and often eliminates creativity of the leadership team. Cost-based managers often respond to new opportunity-based ideas with phrases like, "We can't do that, we could never get the funds to pay for it." All the while, they continue to promote nearly any idea to reduce cost. Many of the cost-reduction efforts look good in isolation but ultimately result in losses through unrecognized ripple effects and trade-offs.

You can envision these ripple effects and trade-offs by thinking about trying to solve Rubik's Cube. Without a solution, most people solve one side of the cube first, making one perfect side. Think about what happens when they solve that one side. All of the other sides are changing, and none of them are getting closer to their perfect combination. This is the same thing that happens to a team when each member is focused on his or her own departments without recognizing ripple effects of their decisions.

Full-Context Decision-Making

Best-possible decision-making is simply not possible without full-context decision-support technologies. The traditional act of simplifying complex decisions (to accommodate our human limitations), often by assuming everything stays fixed beyond the issue at hand, produces out-of-context decisions that cost bottom-line profits.

Whether about delivering service, addressing constraints, or acquiring and allocating resources, complex decisions are ever present. The most common practice today is still to rely on spreadsheet-based decision-making that is unable to recognize and consider inevitable interactions, trade-offs, and upstream and downstream ripple effects that are associated with all decisions.

It is impossible to aim at your BestPossible if you don't know what it is, or what the profit gap between it and current performance is.

The Profit Gap

Profit gaps, the difference between what you could be making and what you're currently making, are a fact of life. Because of business complexities—constantly changing circumstances that overwhelm human comprehension and the natural limits of organizational responsiveness—there will always be a gap between where companies stand and where they could be in terms of achieving their full potential. The good news is that a company's profit gap is, in fact, also its *field of opportunities* (see Figure 5.1). Every opportunity for better performance resides here—there is no other place to look.

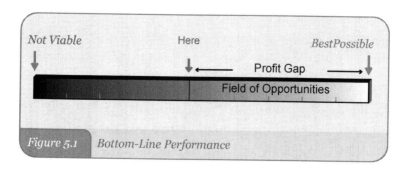

Figure 5.1   *Bottom-Line Performance*

It is impossible to aim at your BestPossible if you don't know what it is, or what the profit gap between it and current performance is.

Team Commitment

Perhaps the most important element of the game is getting and keeping all players on the same playbook. Misalignments bring discord resulting in wasted energy and resources. Maintaining congruence among strategies, tactics, and operations is always challenging but is made a lot easier with a common playbook—an enterprise model designed to recognize and coordinate all aspects of the company.

When team members doubt the plans they are pursuing, they tend to "comply" rather than "commit," and thus stifling progress.

When team members doubt the plans they are pursuing, they tend to "comply" rather than "commit," and thus stifling progress, perpetuating misalignment, and reducing the ability to capture new opportunities. When each leader on the team agrees with the level of flexibility they have and recognize the EO plans are truly the best-possible for the whole of the business, full commitment becomes the norm.

Constraint Management

All companies have profit constraints, or they would have infinite earnings.

For all practical purposes, there are no insurmountable constraints—they can all be relieved with sharp focus and creativity.

A client once challenged this by pointing to time as a hard constraint with only twenty-four hours in a day. However, one of his colleagues quickly objected by saying "If we want more than twenty-four hours of production, we can build or buy another plant."

Most constraints come in the form of limited capital, procurement options, production capabilities, and/or market opportunities. The Profit Hawk is able to identify the most limiting constraints and prioritize them to deliberately overcome them.

Success depends on your company's ability to identify and serve your sweet spot.

Customer Service

Whatever a company's mission, it must inevitably be delivering value in service of customer needs. As described later, *market opportunities* constitute every company's foundational resource. It follows that your company's level of success is highly dependent on how well you choose target markets and which customers to serve within those markets.

The goal is to align your resources to optimally serve the needs of your chosen markets and then sell product and service mixes that make best-possible use of your production capabilities. High-level success depends on your company's ability to identify and serve your sweet spot under continually changing market conditions.

Business Management

Business management is more demanding and complex than we like to admit. The basic elements already discussed illustrate why your full potential is not achievable without applying optimization to integrate and coordinate all aspects of your decision environment.

Many companies have installed extensive data collection and storage systems, believing that more complete, readily accessible data would enable better decisions. Unfortunately, without tools to distill numbers into pertinent information, more data can make good decisions more difficult and doing wrong things better is a very real risk.

Best-possible performance is all about doing the right things in the right amounts at the right times.

Best-possible performance is all about doing the right things in the right amounts at the right times. Profit Hawks are prepared to analyze, plan, schedule, execute, monitor, and adjust activities to help achieve your best-possible results.

Q *GIGO–garbage in, garbage out. If we don't have good data, how can we trust the model's results?*

A You are currently making decisions and running things based on whatever numbers you have and based on assumptions and experience. Those same numbers, assumptions, and experiences can be captured and put into an LP model and then tested, refined, and controlled to yield full-context guidance and better results. Without profit modeling as a place to test and use good data, bad data are likely to stay bad, with unrecognized consequences.

Most importantly, the decisions you are making today are not as good as those you would be making with even a simple model. The saying within the LP modeling discipline is this: you are better off being approximately right than being precisely wrong.

A preliminary model can be developed quickly to capitalize on the knowledge and experience of the leadership team and any available hard data to provide directionally correct plans to increase profits. As the profit sensitivity of business elements becomes known, data collection can be improved to refine the model.

Chapter 6

Offense Wins Games

Who hasn't watched a football or soccer team with a late-game lead go into "prevent-defense"? Many now refer to it as the "prevent-a-win defense." We can all see it. The team with the lead goes into a defensive mode and often loses because the other team gets more creative and stays on the offensive, where nearly all scoring occurs.

The same holds true for enterprise growth. When on defense, we are, at best, maintaining. When on offense, we are creative and can give it our all. We can produce growth. In the game of Enterprise Optimization, offense-based creativity wins every time; with better tools we can be more creative and become better players.

Where is most of your decision-making right now?

Rather than defending past successes, this is about continually exploring, identifying, and capturing new opportunities…winning with our offense.

Four Modes of Leadership

On offense, we seek pleasure; on defense, we work to avoid pain. For both, we act either creatively or systematically. When we think and act creatively and offensively, and we reject the deceptive short-term security of cost-based management (CBM), we are practicing offense-based leadership (OBL). This involves systematically tapping into our fields of opportunities. Rather than defending past successes, this is about continually exploring, identifying, and capturing new opportunities ahead of us—winning with our offense.

Offense has historically been viewed as higher risk than defense but with greater rewards. However, today's EO technology mitigates the risks and enhances the rewards of offense-based management. The most effective leaders and Profit Hawks focus on cycling between mode 1 and mode 2, the two offensive modes (see Figure 6.1). Even as plans are being executed, new and better plans and tactics are being explored and created. The Profit Hawk is the catalyst and champion of this practice.

All companies start life in the *innovative mode* (offensively creative). They then naturally move into the *progressive mode* where we systematically put our innovations into action. At some point, they slip quietly and often unintentionally into the *protective mode* (systematically defensive) where they protect their successes and stay with what they know worked in the past.

Profit Hawks spend their time working in the offensive modes of strategic planning and being proactive whenever possible.

Mode 1—Creative Offense

Creative offense, when paired with mode 2, systematic offense is where Enterprise Optimization offers the greatest leverage for profit improvements. Great tools enable great leadership. By allowing company leaders to see clearly where their opportunities reside, and to prioritize the efforts

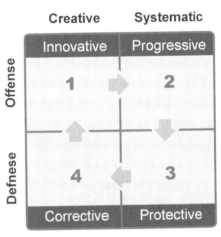

Figure 6.1 Modes of Leadership

through the use of all-things-considered *opportunities values* (explained in chapter 10, The Science), they are assured of properly focused efforts and optimal plans.

Mode 2—Systematic Offense

The fully integrated and coordinated *departmental road maps* (integrated plans) of Enterprise Optimization assure all aspects of operational activities are implemented in congruence with planned strategies and tactics. When new constraints appear, as they inevitably do, the systems facilitate immediate course corrections.

Mode 3—Systematic Defense

When on stabilizing protective defense, Enterprise Optimization works to identify and quantify profit-limiting effects of outdated policies, practices, and traditions. EO also ensures a systematic approach to recovering from a defensive position.

Mode 4—Creative Defense

Unexpected problems, breakdowns, and crises happen. When they happen, quick use of Enterprise Optimization systems can facilitate creative and timely solutions. Crisis management is a strong suit of EO technology because it generates creativity by clearly pointing out the constraints and opportunities available.

We can imagine things that we can do, and we can do things that we can imagine.

Envisioning Success

We can imagine things that we can do, and we can do things that we can imagine. This may not always be true, but it is a good rule of thumb to start developing an exciting vision of the future. Consider a football team that simply wants to consistently achieve a 50 percent winning percentage, year after year. What is the probability that they will find the motivation and commitment necessary to win a championship? Yet many leaders inadvertently set the same type of vision for their companies.

Envisioning a better future is a job for upper management, with CEOs as team leaders and where Profit Hawks provide the road maps and feedback. Starting from a foundation of what we know to be working well, practicing the art of Enterprise Optimization is an exercise of molding and shaping an ever-improving vision for the journey ahead.

To be effective, a vision must be believable, motivational, inspirational, and achievable. Our current perspectives determine what we deem to be possible. We don't pursue what we can't see. But it doesn't matter that our visions are currently limited—as we apply EO systems to pursue new opportunities, more opportunities will come into view to make today's Best-Possible better tomorrow.

With near-infinite possibilities to consider, creating optimal visions of the future may seem daunting, if not impossible, but that kind of thinking is what limits many. If you have gained anything up to this point, you will not limit yourself simply because an opportunity seems daunting. You will use your EO tools and support your Profit Hawks to motivate your team's growth.

Q *We are an "operationally driven" company. How does an EO system apply to what we can do as a sales team?*

A When a company sees itself as "operationally driven," it generally means they are focused on cost-based management and are likely focused on the measurement of cost per product and revenue. With the traditional tools and these measures sometimes seen as the only realities, it is understandable and common to be efficiency-driven.

However, when even the staunchest cost-based leader sees the opportunity to sell a better mix, even at the expense of production efficiency for more overall profit, decision-making will start to shift. BestPossible is only achieved when there is optimally balanced planning based on the market opportunities at the time.

Sales must strive to book orders that optimize the use of company capabilities, pulling production to make what's right. As production pushes to improve efficiencies on certain desirable products, the sales mix that is right for the enterprise will continue to change.

Chapter 7

The Five Game Pieces

One of the most detrimental business norms is the persistent belief that we should stay out of each other's area of responsibility. That can work in sports, using football as an example again, the coaches of the offense, defense and special teams can build their strategies and tactics independently and still succeed.

In business it is impossible to even envision your Best-Possible without integrating all of your options for your five game pieces. For example, operation-minded companies can never excel without optimizing what they offer to their markets, or who they choose to be a part of their markets (sales).

The decisions made in each area of responsibility have inevitable consequences on the others and they impact the bottom-line. We all know that if left to chance these are more likely to be negative than positive.

Every game requires some form of equipment or playing pieces. In the game of Enterprise Optimization, there are five game pieces. All pieces are necessary to play, and no others can be substituted. They are your five basic resources:

1. Capital
2. Procurement options
3. Sales opportunities
4. Production capabilities
5. Information

There can be no advancement without change, and there can be no change without the use of resources. This means the process of Enterprise Optimization is really about the procurement and use of these resources. EO recognizes all big-picture effects while leading to choices and decisions of maximum advantage.

We advance by the strengths of our resources and our skills in using them. To advance substantially, we must add to our strengths and our skills.

As we work to optimize our operations, we need to look beyond existing resources to include those we can acquire. We advance by the strengths of our resources and our skills in using them. To advance substantially, we must add to our strengths and our skills.

Capital

The key resource in the world of business is capital—how we use our dollars affects the availability and latent value of all other resources. Therefore, capital is the basic resource that makes all others possible. We need money to acquire information, to gain access to market opportunities to buy and sell things, and to acquire production capabilities. This puts acquiring and allocating capital among our most important activities.

[EO] systems are uniquely capable of...clearly showing where to deploy capital for greater returns.

Enterprise Optimization systems are uniquely capable of supporting strategic planning, clearly showing where to deploy capital for greater returns. They are also great for justifying and attracting new capital.

Procurement Options

Once we have capital, we can procure space, production capabilities, human resources, raw materials, and customers. From the very beginning, tapping into the right procurement opportunities is critical to profits, growth, and long-term success.

Our optimal mix of procurement options changes with market conditions and with changes within and among our other four resource categories. Everything is interrelated, and resource changes affect our bottom-line profits in complex ways. Again, the sweet spot of every enterprise includes the in-context optimization of current procurement options.

Sales Opportunities

For most companies, sales constraints are their most confining and profit-limiting and traditionally include the most difficult-to-overcome self-imposed constraints. Although many leaders do not think of sales opportunities as resources, they are. In fact, the sales team is a critical and finite resource, as is its pool of current and potential customers.

Remember, a resource is anything we can use to achieve a purpose. If the purpose of our business is to create and serve customers, acquiring and tapping into market opportunities is what gives meaning to the application of all other resources.

Too often, we start to believe and perpetuate the paradigm that we really don't have much choice when it comes to the orders we get. You've surely said or heard, "At times like these, we have to take every order we can get." But consider this: unless we have 100 percent market share for every product we offer, we have room to maneuver. Even if we have a 50 percent market share for an offering, we still have 50 percent of room to maneuver, and it is likely that within that 50 percent is more of our sweet spot.

An equally limiting paradigm is this thinking: "Our sales team is already selling everything it can, at the best price they can." Every sales professional knows this is the goal, but never achieved. The primary reason it is not possible is that most sales personnel have no way of knowing what their optimal sales mix is. That leaves them making decisions on how and when they will pursue sales based on their own experience, often leading to the best-volume customers and not to the most profitable in the context of the whole enterprise.

Down markets can provide the best opportunities for proactive prospecting, pricing, and selling. Such opportunities unfold while and because competition is hunkering down or doing business as usual.

Companies…focusing on sales volume in hopes of improving profits invariably have significant profit opportunities available.

Product mix is always a key controllable variable, and the most limiting paradigm of all is "volume keeps the lights on." Companies that still think this way, focusing on sales volume in hopes of improving profits, invariably have significant profit opportunities available in product mix, regardless of their current levels of success.

Production Capabilities

This category of resources includes everything we have available to produce products and provide services: human resources, utilities, inventories, space, equipment, outsourcing options, information, and procurement options for all of these.
Production involves a lot more than converting raw materials and delivering products and services. It includes engaging employees, attending to safety issues, satisfying customers, building

teams, protecting assets, and managing leadership roles in all elements of the business processes.

Information

Identifying and realizing opportunities requires information. We need tools that can create and present optimization-based information. Visions born of fact-based knowledge serve to deliver us from stifling defense to pursue profitable offense. The right information propels us beyond our current perceptions and self-imposed limitations.

Five leadership activities are particularly information-critical: (1) planning, (2) scheduling, (3) executing, (4) monitoring, and (5) navigating. Of these, planning, scheduling, and navigating require integration of information and are where we will find our most profitable opportunities for improvement.

These activities and their attendant information are necessary to identify opportunities within all three time-based planning horizons: strategic, tactical, and operational. They also apply to all three fundamental business functions: procurement, production, and sales. With so many layers and permutations, it is easy to see why the ability to make timely, accurate navigational adjustments in response to mounting complexities is so powerful.

Q *Linear programming has been around a long time, why hasn't EO taken off already?*

A It has, but its takeoff has been slow because of lack of recognized need and broad awareness.

With advancements in mainframe computers in the 1960s, LP soon became widely used by progressive companies. However, because traditional management structures and focus were (and still are) departmentalized, most applications were aimed at individual functions—consequently, suboptimizing the enterprise.

The term *Enterprise Optimization* was coined by Dr. Eugene L. Bryan (coauthor of this book) in 1970 to label his use of LP to optimize all company functions (procurement, production, and sales) for best-possible bottom-line performance. Dr. Bryan has equipped and trained dozens of major corporations and hundreds of smaller companies to reap the rewards of EO.

Today, EO is applied worldwide, but its use is still relatively limited. This is quickly changing as the capability for better decision-making becomes more obvious and as early adopters gain overwhelming competitive advantages.

Chapter 8

Field of Opportunities

How ready are you to declare that your company is as profitable as it can possibly be? If you are picking up what we have tried to share to this point in the book, you will recognize that's a loaded question.

Even if you are achieving extraordinary results, you know that there are opportunities available to you. You might not have exposed them yet, but there will always be a field of opportunities for your business.

Accepting the humbling and yet motivating reality that opportunities exist is a critical step, then you need your team's creativity and intelligence to identify them.

Where are your biggest opportunities right now?

The difference between our current performance and your Best-Possible is our *profit gap* and where all of our business growth can occur—to put it more positively, our *field of opportunities.*

Several important categories of opportunities are available to Profit Hawks as they work to identify and achieve their companies' best-possible performance.

How we see ourselves ultimately determines our levels of success…because our perceptions precondition our expectations.

Inside the Box

How we see ourselves ultimately determines our levels of success…because our perceptions precondition our expectations. This is why the paradigms we craft are so important—they set limits on our levels of success. They stake out what we believe to be possible. Our paradigms are our identities. Because we live with constant change, our identities must remain works in progress if we are to stay ready to dodge threats and recognize unfolding opportunities.

For example, one of our clients was promoted to lead a major division of a steel company and faced an immediate challenge. His company's CEO promoted him to the position and explained that there was little or no chance of making the operations profitable. Therefore, his responsibility was to slow the bleeding as much as possible. The division had failed to turn a profit in six years and they had tried everything, always with an excuse—a limiting paradigm accepted by the company.

However, within eighteen months, the newly promoted leader was able to change the prevailing paradigms. He harnessed optimization science as a tool to identify the actual potential of the division and to engage the demotivated and skeptical staff.

His division soon turned a profit, and even through the throes of a deep recession, his division became the most profitable in the entire company. As of this writing, the division has achieved continued profitability.

The art of optimization includes inside-the-box development of new and improved expectations, processes, and products along with innovative leadership and team development. Inside-the-box opportunities are sitting right in front of us every day.

Traditions and Perceptions

We unwittingly create paradigms through our traditions, experiences, and perceptions—inside-the-box thinking (see Figure 8.1). We think, plan, and act within what we see as our limits of operations and according to policies and practices we believe necessary to be successful within those limits. When we can see and act beyond our paradigms, we act differently and have fewer self-imposed restrictions; we are more innovative.

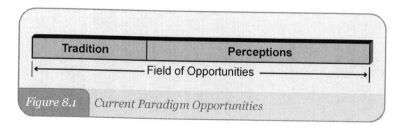

Figure 8.1   Current Paradigm Opportunities

However, we need assistance to do so because others think they are already doing the right things, or they would be doing different things. This is much more than a circular argument; it explains comfort zones and the natural resistance to change. This is a root cause of many business failures.

Traditions are not inherently bad. In fact, they play vital roles as they provide stability and guidance. But in a world of rapid change, it is critical to balance stability with advancement and bold exploration.

We have opportunities for improvement within the traditions and perceptions of our current paradigms. In fact, with or without EO technology, this is where we will often find our most immediate opportunities. By challenging our perceived limits, we open doors to fresh opportunities. It is through this process that we make tomorrow's BestPossible better than today's.

The most effective leaders are in business for the long haul and realize that quick gains made at the expense of long-term health are false gains. Exceptions may be necessary for dealing with pending cash-flow crises, but as we pursue low-cost, near-term opportunities, we should always question if our activities are building strength for long-term success.

Outside the Box

As surely as we can confine ourselves with self-imposed walls and rules, we can just as surely liberate ourselves by thinking outside the box. It is important to realize that there will always be too many offensive opportunities to pursue to waste time and resources on defensive efforts.

What we have always done, what the competition is and has been doing, what we think our customers and suppliers need—these are all beliefs that we can lock ourselves into. The concept of searching outside the box requires us to rethink our beliefs about our market and our approach to business. What worked yesterday may be inadequate today. Hanging on to what worked yesterday as a safe approach is classically defensive and is, therefore, prone to be limiting if not detrimental.

Imagining and exploring these opportunities is the responsibility of the senior leadership. Testing these outside-of-the-box opportunities and creating the plans that would achieve these opportunities is the job of the Profit Hawk.

Simple Opportunities

Within our fields of opportunities are single-issue, simple opportunities—meaning they offer advantages independent of big-picture considerations. Keep in mind that simple opportunities are not necessarily easy, and complex opportunities aren't necessarily difficult.

> *We spend inordinate amounts of time and money
> on better execution, and not enough time questioning
> the initiatives we are executing.*

Simple opportunities involve single objectives such as lowering the cost of a process, improving productivity, reducing waste, or improving quality. They most often relate to execution. Unfortunately, because doing things better is the most obvious way to improve, we spend inordinate amounts of time and money on better execution, and not enough time questioning the initiatives we are executing.

Simple opportunities offer independent value with single units of measure (such as dollars, hours, or volume). Initiatives such as total quality management (TQM), statistical process control (SPC), just-in-time inventory management (JIT), lean manufacturing, and process automation all aim at simple opportunities. Although such undertakings can substantially improve earnings and competitive positions, they remain stand-alone initiatives that offer incremental improvements that may or may not produce big gains.

Consider this example: Improving productivity of an underused work center may reduce payroll costs or free up personnel for assignments elsewhere. In contrast, performance improvement at a work center identified as a systemwide bottleneck can add to company output, reduce overall production costs, and dramatically increase profit margins.

A word of caution: If not done optimally, cutting costs can lead to the disproportionate loss of revenue, goodwill, and competitive position. For example, reducing costs by scaling back workforce and related service offerings can put a struggling company out of business.

Company executives have historically aimed much of their planning and capital at simple opportunities. One reason is that most requests for capital spending come from line managers rewarded on simple opportunities such as productivity and lower costs. To change the thought processes and focus to enterprise performance, leadership must align incentives accordingly.

More lucrative, complex opportunities can involve nothing more than a few adjustments in strategies, tactics, practices, or policies.

Keep in mind that capturing simple opportunities often requires major capital expenditures, while much more lucrative, complex opportunities can involve nothing more than a few adjustments in strategies, tactics, practices, or policies.

Complex Opportunities

Complex opportunities can come from minor changes of plans and policies that can offer dramatic results. A key role of the Profit Hawk is to actively seek out these opportunities with their specialized skills, understanding, and tool kit.

It usually costs less to rethink the business than to squeeze more out of what we are already doing. Finding and targeting complex opportunities are planning functions aimed at doing the right things in the right amounts at the right times. Complex opportunities dominate our fields of opportunities because they are more:

- *Plentiful.* They lie hidden by their own complexities, and they remain mostly untapped. We haven't gone after what we haven't seen.

- *Valuable.* There is more bottom-line advantage in doing the right things than in doing wrong things better.

Complexity becomes a good thing when we acquire the tools and gain the skills to expose them within our fields of opportunities. Ironically, many complex opportunities are quite easy to capture once we see them, but without an optimization system, they are hard to find among near-infinite possible patterns of activities. Seemingly minor big-picture adjustments can significantly improve bottom-line results.

To add to the best of opportunities and potential for more profits, we need to add flexibility and complexity.

Especially during tough times, there is temptation to reduce complexity and perceived risks by reducing numbers of product and service offerings. The brutal irony is that simplification often works directly against bottom-line profits. Our most lucrative opportunities are complex, in good times and bad. This means if we are to add to the best of opportunities and potential for more profits, we need to add flexibility and complexity.

This is counter to conventional wisdom and even counter-intuitive, but true nonetheless. A company offering a single product in one size and color, or one type of service to one type of customer, will never be able to match the profit potentials of more diversified competitors.

Nine Cells of Opportunities

Because opportunities are literally endless, they can be over-whelming for decision-makers. For this reason, we often miss the best opportunities while going after the most obvious. To improve the process, we need a way to effectively identify and prioritize our opportunities. An effective method to consider is what we call the Nine Cells of Opportunities.

The Nine Cells helps everyone better understand their field of opportunities. By helping to identify, classify, and prioritize opportunities for profit improvement, your team can quickly get behind the most important opportunities (see Figure 8.2).

Although individual cells contain simple opportunities to in-dependently improve earnings through better execution, much bigger gains will come from optimally balancing the three cells of a given row of the table. For example, strategic adjustments within and among cells 1, 2, and 3 will have the most highly leveraged effects on long-term profits.

	Procurement	Production	Sales
Strategic	Cell 1	Cell 2	Cell 3
Tactical	Cell 4	Cell 5	Cell 6
Operational	Cell 7	Cell 8	Cell 9

Figure 8.2   *The Nine Cells of Opportunity*

Tactical maneuvering within cells 4, 5, and 6 offers the best avenue for early advances. Here, optimal adjustments of procurement, production, and sales activities within current strategies will leverage existing production capabilities for major profit improvements.

Although important, operational planning usually offers less opportunity for profit improvement than tactical planning. Cells 7, 8, and 9 are where things start happening shortly after or even during the planning process. For this reason, operational planning must focus mainly on getting the job done and is usually a primary strength of most companies.

Strategy defines *what* will be done, tactics define the *how* and *where*, while operational planning looks after the *here* and *now* of execution. The better we execute, the more we gain from our tactics and strategies. That is why BestPossible profits come from keeping all nine cells in balance.

Strategies, Tactics, Operations

Opportunities always pertain to the future—be it tomorrow, next month, next year, or whatever relevant time horizon. Business planning can be strategic, tactical, or operational, and one type must always recognize and consider the other two.

- Strategic planning involves positioning operations for long-term success by lining up resources and providing flexibility to pursue new and changing markets. Strategies are about what we do over the long term and involve the most significant investments in growth-related resources. Because they always entail risk, strategies call for fact-based decision-making and support.

- Tactical planning is for maneuvering within chosen strategies in light of changing operational capabilities, flexibilities, and unfolding opportunities. Tactics are about investments in resources to support and facilitate strategies. They are shorter term, more flexible, and less risky than strategies.

- Operational planning is for near-term execution of strategy-based tactics. These rarely involve capital investments, are very flexible, and are about today's and tomorrow's results. They are immediate and pose minimal risk. This type of planning is where the rubber meets the road and where decisions are made that affect today's results (see Figure 8.3).

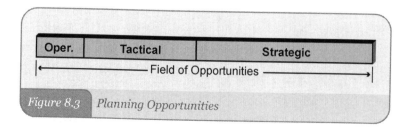

Figure 8.3   *Planning Opportunities*

Figure 8.3 illustrates the relative size of the profit opportunities of each planning horizon with operational planning being the smallest and strategic planning usually offering the greatest room for improvement.

Beyond routine scheduling, operational planning is for improving the way we get things done. While always important, operational planning (doing things right) offers less bottom-line advantage than optimal strategies and tactics (doing the right things).

It is important to recognize that operational planning can result in the inadvertent losses of profits when such efforts are done out of context and independent of other efforts. This is suboptimization that happens when one department optimizes their performance rather than working in concert with all departments—solving one side of Rubik's Cube without respect to the other sides.

Next in order of profit leverage is tactical planning, which is where we maneuver within company strategies to gain advantage from or defend against external changes. Tactical adjustments are in the near term (for example, next month, next quarter), between changes in strategies.

Strategic planning is most important and typically offers the greatest bottom-line advantage, yet is the least common in companies that are locked into defensive, cost-based management. In fact, many companies define their strategic plan as a capital plan for the next year.

Procurement, Production, Sales

Within each of our three planning horizons, we have opportunities for profit improvements within and among our three primary business functions (see Figure 8.4):

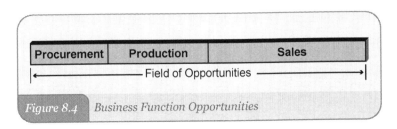

Figure 8.4 *Business Function Opportunities*

Procurement—we have opportunities for sourcing and acquiring better resources including capital, services of new employees, vendors, materials, space, and equipment. In today's terms, supply-chain management addresses many procurement functions, but not all.

Production—these are opportunities to add greater value through better use of internally and externally available production capabilities and for innovative research and development of new offerings.

Sales—here we are talking about market opportunities that allow a more rewarding use of procurement options and production capabilities. Of special note, sales opportunities include engaging in R&D activities aimed at creating brands so that the company and its products and services can be distinguished from pure-commodity offerings.

Note that the sales segment is larger than the other two. For most industries, improved sales mixes offer major opportunities for more profitable procurement and production.

Q *We're in a commodity business with little control of product pricing. We can easily calculate profit margins and sell accordingly. Do we really need this system to sell effectively?*

A Accounting-based, profit-margin calculations rely on too many faulty assumptions and are misleading at the product and customer level. At best, they provide crude estimates of relative value. With EO guidance that recognizes all trade-offs and ripple effects that invariably affect bottom-line results, you will be able to continuously adjust to the best-possible products, service levels, and pricing. The optimally profitable mix is an elusive, dynamic target that can't be determined from a single snapshot in time.

In addition, even in commodity markets, when the "good" customers buy products, they look for quality and service. They will pay only so much for the "commodity," but will pay more for the quality and service they want—by definition that makes them "good" customers, if you are willing to understand their needs and be the best supplier.

Chapter 9

The New Scoreboard

John E. Jones wrote, "What gets measured gets done; what gets measured and fed back gets done well; what gets rewarded gets repeated."

With that in mind, consider the goals, measurements, compensation/incentive plans, and personal recognition that has driven your business prior to implementing EO.

You probably already realize that you can't keep measuring, and rewarding the same and expect to get better results. The game has changed and so must the scoreboard.

Fair warning—the paradigms around compensation programs are some of the most sensitive "sacred-cows" we have encountered on the path to EO. Fortunately, as sensitive as these issues may be, we have found that most people will pursue "what's right" even while there is some cost to them, people are motivated by winning.

Every leader with a passion for being the best has struggled with the measurements of their performance. We know that leaders often do their best work when confronting tough market conditions, where the traditional measures often indicate poor performance—lower profits. We also know that with far less effort, and sometimes by blind luck, during up-market conditions, we can be seen as exemplary leaders with those very same measures—higher profits.

EO system's new scoreboards change the traditional measures forever, and an important role of Profit Hawks is to understand and help leadership teams apply these new metrics to accelerate progress.

Properly measuring performance requires that we recognize that our company's profits are a function of two primary factors, market, and leadership. So to measure and ensure progress, we need to isolate and monitor the controllable factor of leadership. Just as a sailboat experiences winds and currents from different directions and speeds requiring course adjustments to reach its destination, if we fail to understand the forces acting on our business, we can't stay on an optimal course. We have to mitigate the forces working against us and capitalize on forces that enhance our bottom line.

External market drivers include material costs, wage rates, energy prices, and product prices. Although external factors are usually beyond our direct control, we can change how they affect us by creatively changing how we operate and who we buy from and sell to within our external business environments.

Companies traditionally monitor indicators such as manufacturing cost and labor hours per unit of production, which are of value for avoiding and correcting problems. The monthly income statements are of little value as measures of leadership team performance; they don't indicate how well we are doing relative to our markets for buying and selling goods and services.

The new scoreboard monitors and reports what's most import to company success. In addition to normally calculated profits, the new scoreboard reports the following:

- Profit performance independent of changes in market prices
- How close the business is to achieving its full potential
- How well each leader performed to his or her part of optimized plans
- How creative leaders have been at overcoming profit constraints

Normalized Performance Tracking

Once in use, your operation's EO scoreboard (Figure 9.1) and all related performance indices (Figures 9.2, 9.3, and 9.4) will filter out (normalize) effects of market cycles to display how well your leaders are doing with what they can control. It is based on two critical values: *normalized profits* and *normalized BestPossible profits* for each tracking period—typically each month of a company's fiscal year.

The new scoreboard includes each period's normalized (market-adjusted) profit relative to the company's chosen baseline period (December in our example) to represent a "good period" of performance. A value of 0 percent means that, without the market influences, leadership actions kept pace with the baseline performance, and they produced no improvement or decline.

The second value, normalized BestPossible profit, is a calcu-
lation of the optimal bottom-line profit based on each month's
procurement, production, and sales constraints. The constraints
are those established by the leaders as their input to the optimization system run. The growth in BestPossible profits is the
result of leadership creatively overcoming constraints alone, not
market effects.

Because LP constraints are imposed by the leaders responsi-
ble for making things happen, resulting targets are more credible
than traditionally set goals, such as "stretch goals."

By constraining the analysis to the current opportunities, capabilities, and limitations, the resulting optimal profit is a clear,
achievable target for next month's or any future period's earnings. Remember, optimal means best-possible, which means it is
doable—all things considered.

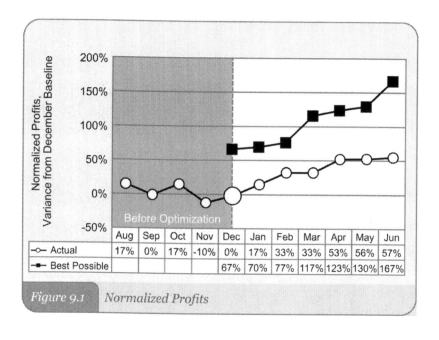

	Aug	Sep	Oct	Nov	Dec	Jan	Feb	Mar	Apr	May	Jun
—o— Actual	17%	0%	17%	-10%	0%	17%	33%	33%	53%	56%	57%
—■— Best Possible					67%	70%	77%	117%	123%	130%	167%

Figure 9.1   Normalized Profits

Performance Index

As market prices and costs change, so do profits. However, market-driven price and cost changes are not usually uniform among products or geographical regions. Individual product prices and material and service costs move up and down according to market forces.

Disproportional price and cost movements always create opportunities for advantageous product-mix adjustments. In fact, there is nearly always a product-mix adjustment with every new analysis.

The Performance Index (Figure 9.2) illustrates the normalized relationship of *actual* profit over *baseline* profits.

In this example, the departure of the Performance Index from the baseline over the first six months of benchmarking is a direct result of better decisions, clear views of the opportunities, and integrated plans to get there.

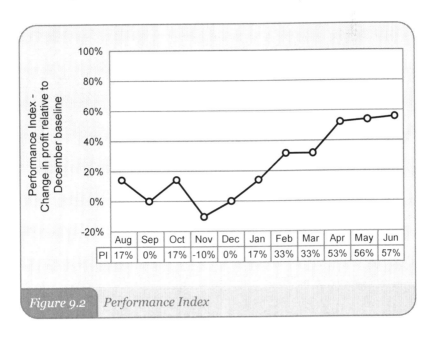

	Aug	Sep	Oct	Nov	Dec	Jan	Feb	Mar	Apr	May	Jun
PI	17%	0%	17%	-10%	0%	17%	33%	33%	53%	56%	57%

Figure 9.2 *Performance Index*

Achievement Index

The Achievement Index (AI) (Figure 9.3) is each month's profit as a percentage of the month's optimal target. The initial AI in December, when the process was first used to identify a *Best-Possible* plan, showed a 60 percent achievement, or a 40 percent opportunity for improvement.

The message here is that without recognizing opportunities within their current constraints and capabilities, they were only achieving 60 percent of what they now realized was possible.

However, by February the AI of 75 percent means that the team was able to achieve 75 percent of that month's potential profit. Keep in mind that the team's BestPossible profit, its potential, has also increased as has their level of achievement toward it. The increased potential can be seen in the *Creativity Index* discussed next. This is a typical result of the initial use of EO systems.

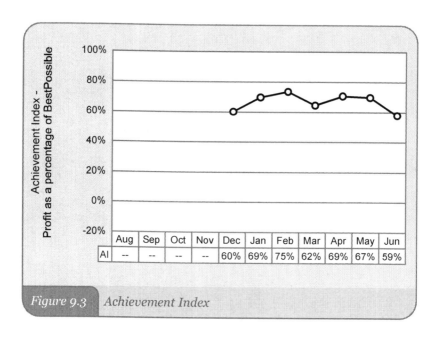

	Aug	Sep	Oct	Nov	Dec	Jan	Feb	Mar	Apr	May	Jun
AI	--	--	--	--	60%	69%	75%	62%	69%	67%	59%

Figure 9.3   *Achievement Index*

Creativity Index

The Creativity Index (CI) (Figure 9.4) illustrates each month's gain (or loss) in the company's BestPossible profit relative to the baseline profit value. Using February as an example, the results show that the leadership team has been able to identify and overcome enough constraints and/or create new opportunities to add 6 percent to their original profit potential.

June's Creativity Index of 60 percent means the company's leaders were able to find ways to overcome enough constraints and/or create new products and services from their *field of opportunities* to add 60 percent to their original best-possible profit potential over the first six months of the year.

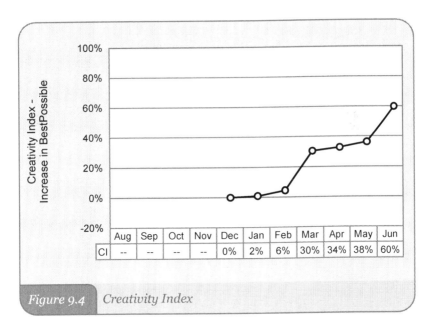

	Aug	Sep	Oct	Nov	Dec	Jan	Feb	Mar	Apr	May	Jun
CI	--	--	--	--	0%	2%	6%	30%	34%	38%	60%

Figure 9.4   *Creativity Index*

Creativity opens doors to new opportunities; this is the nature of offense-based management. Progressive leaders will find ways to make profitable events happen when they know what exciting possibilities can be achieved.

Q *What good will it do us to know that we should sell a different mix of products? Our market is always changing, and we don't control it.*

A Most sales professionals recognize that they can control some portion of their sales by applying their limited time and resources to the customers who tend to buy a certain type or mix of products and services. These professionals have developed their practices and processes to do what they believe is best.

When they have the right information to adjust their plans, nearly every sales professional will be able to make at least a 2 to 5 percent change in their sales mix over a sales cycle. As the sales personnel become accustomed to making these changes, they become more efficient and effective and guard against actions that limit their flexibility, all of which increase their ability to grow profits.

Chapter 10

The Science of EO

The basic question for all business leaders is: "What do we need to do to achieve our vision under the continually changing conditions?"

This specific question is seldom asked. Most leadership teams approach the question obliquely, looking to be better wherever they can. You will often hear concerns and complaints about constant change, thought of as a burden to the business and growth.

Most leaders inherently recognize that the systems they have aren't effectively answering the basic question and that they certainly aren't able to deal with the changes efficiently.

The science of EO was developed with that specific question in mind. It not only answers the question, it turns the continuous change into a source of continuous opportunity.

The beauty of EO systems is that software technology has progressed to the point that users no longer need to bother themselves with how it works. Just as the sailboat captain doesn't need to know how his or her GPS is able to accurately pinpoint their location in the middle of the ocean, neither do business leaders nor Profit Hawks need to know how the optimization systems do their magic to get the results.

However, many of us Profit Hawk–types truly enjoy the technical side and the elegance of a user-friendly system. If you are one of us or just curious, this section is intended for you.

With all of our technological advancements, it is unfortunate that most companies still rely on cost-based methods for business planning. Even though many use advanced data storage and retrieval, inventory management, requirements-planning, and supply-chain systems, these are essentially high-tech tools created to reduce and control costs in support of traditional cost-based management; they are not optimization technologies able to lead the way to best-possible performance.

Optimization Systems

Management tools will continue to evolve. There will always be reasons and ways to improve them. Although we will surely find better ways to harness and apply Enterprise Optimization technology, it's hard to imagine a better management tool than one that shows in detail how good we can be and what we need to do to make it our reality.

The creative-planning side of business is more art than science, but better tools make better artists. The more quickly we can spot opportunities and test ideas, the better our decisions and greater our progress.

We now use optimization technologies to identify and prioritize previously hidden opportunities at mind-boggling speeds. EO systems facilitate business planning, in the same way GPS systems facilitate geographical navigation. Just as GPS applications for cars now call on real-time traffic data for best-route guidance, LP-based profit optimization systems use current data to generate optimal-profit road maps. They let us see where we are, what is possible, and what we need to do to "get there from here."

How It All Works

Optimization is not as mystifying as it might seem. Because LP models mirror known decision environments, their features are clearly recognizable. They use familiar data, follow familiar activities, and are constrained to honor company realities.

The systems work to maximize spreads between net revenues and cost of sales. This happens in one of three ways (see Table 10.1):

	Net Revenues	Cost of Sales	Profits
1	Up	Same or Down	Up
2	Up	Up by less	Up
3	Down	Down by more	Up

Table 10.1

The second is possibly the most important because it is where the system supports offense-based decisions. By reliably determining the return on investments that overcomes current profit constraints, the teams are provided quantitative justifications for capital and for pricing tactics.

The systems operate on a "trial-and-success" methodology for seeking optimal solutions. During sequential iterations, they adjust only those things that will help achieve their objective. In this way, they quickly converge on their objective as they cull out nonoptimal choices without ever moving backward. For profit optimization, they focus on variables that can add to earnings without violating user-imposed ground rules (constraints). In this way, they bypass billions of possibilities as they go straight for the best-possible solution.

Models

Many professions rely on models to test and refine ideas before committing major time and resources. For example, engineers test models of bridges before they build them and process flows before they build new facilities. Models are proving grounds of minimal consequences.

There are two basic classes of computer models for leaders: simulators and optimizers. Simulators accept things as we describe them, to answer "what-if" questions. Optimizers, on the other hand, see things as they could be and give "what's-best" answers for stated objectives.

Optimization models…show the best we can do within the limits of our flexibilities.

Optimization Models

Optimization models serve to create plans, optimize decisions, and enable us to get past our human limitations. Give an optimization system an objective, such as maximized profit, allow it some flexibility, and it will provide the road maps needed to achieve optimal bottom-line results within the reality of procurement, production, sales, and other constraints. They show the best we can do within the limits of our flexibilities and also expose specifically what constrains us for better results.

Two primary components in today's EO systems produce their unique capabilities: linear programming fed with activity-based cost data.

Linear Programming

Linear programming (LP) technology dates back to 1939 when it was developed and ultimately used during World War II for optimal allocations of scarce resources, including materials, equipment, and personnel. Applications varied from developing aerial search patterns to maximizing the chances of finding downed airmen to developing optimal battle strategies.

With the advent of digital computers, LP-based problem solving soon found its way into business applications and, in a rudimentary way, into college classrooms.

As part of the discipline called operations research, LP is widely known among business leaders and executives for its potential benefits. Although industries around the world use LP effectively to deliver solutions, the vast majority of leaders have yet to tap into its most valuable potential—its use as a solver-engine for Enterprise Optimization systems.

As previously described, it doesn't take many interacting variables to yield tens of billions of possible activity patterns. LP-based EO solvers systematically consider and adjust variables, within real-world constraints, until they find the most profitable solutions. Linear programming enables business leaders to make decisions more objectively and with very high confidence.

Today, LP is the most widely used technology for optimizing answers to complex problems. It is now widely used for military planning, for airline scheduling, for supply-chain optimization, and within an ever-growing variety of decision environments.

Activity-Based Costing

In the 1980s, activity-based costing (ABC) was introduced as a solution to the distortions that come with overhead allocations in cost accounting. However, ABC applied independent of optimization, like spreadsheets, relies on isolated analyses where everything beyond the subject at hand is assumed to be fixed, which, of course, is never true.

Just as with conventional costing, ABC has had no way to recognize inevitable trade-offs and internal competition among products for materials, machine time, and sales efforts. Although ABC was a step in the right direction, it needed a way to recognize the full context of the decision environment. We now have that way in the form of linear programming of our EO systems.

From Data to Integrated Plans

Enterprise Optimization systems are more than LP models. To serve as effective decision-making tools for leaders, they require at least four components: (1) data; (2) LP model; (3) LP solver; and (4) reports (see Figure 10.1).

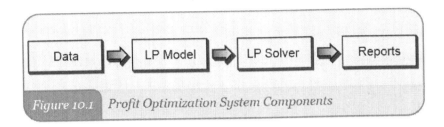

Figure 10.1 *Profit Optimization System Components*

Data

In our high-tech world, data collection and storage have become insidiously easy. We use this negative adjective to caution against the risk of information overload. Companies create elaborate data storage and retrieval systems based on the assumption that people will make better decisions if they have all the data they might need. This is not a valid assumption! Unless we can transform data into useful information, more numbers will only lead to more confusion.

We use data to create information. We analyze information to gain knowledge. We use knowledge to make decisions and control activities. Imploding data into BestPossible knowledge is the work of Enterprise Optimization systems.

The necessary data are limited to these categories:

- Procurement prices/contracts
- Product/service specifications
- Production rates
- Yields
- Sales prices
- Constraints: procurement, production, and sales
- General cost elements

- Consumption rates

Each category involves pure raw data, meaning they come from facts of reality rather than from accounting-based assumptions, manipulations, and allocations. We know the sizes of checks we have to write to buy things and compensate people for doing their work. We know the requirements of products and services we sell. We know how fast they go through required processes and what percentage of a given product meets specs. And finally, we know the sizes of checks we can expect for selling products and services at the market prices.

LP Model

LP models are logic-based arrays of equations that tie all procurement, production, and sales activities together as they relate to each other in real life. For example, it is a reality that when machine time is used, and resources are bought, employees and vendors have to be paid. The logic of a profit model is just as pure as its data and just as easy to understand. Anyone willing to look can plainly see the logic of their operations in their model.

We constrain our model so that it knows what things we have to do and so that it doesn't tell us to produce more than we can sell, or sell more than we can produce. Profit models use constraints to recognize and stay within the confines of the real world, including company policies, regulations, contracts, capacities, and capabilities.

LP Solver

Solvers are programs that accept LP algorithms to simultaneously solve the numerous equations of LP models and perform iterative calculations until solution data sets are produced. The solvers optimize for whatever solution-dependent variable the user chooses, such as net profit. State-of-the-art commercial solvers are able to accomplish massive analyses in the "blink of an eye."

It is a common mistake to assume the advertised capabilities of optimization functions or solvers embedded in spreadsheet or database software are comparable to commercial solvers used in true LP-based profit optimization systems. These add-on capabilities are severely limited in their capacity and are designed to approximate an optimization analysis with much simpler algorithms.

Reports

Reports are custom designed to use solution information produced by the solver and translate it to provide actionable guidance for company leaders. Some of the report content produced with each optimization run includes the following:

- *Pro* forma income statements that show, in detail, how your income statement will look after implementing the current optimal solution.
- Integrated-plan road maps that show what each department/manager is expected to do to coordinate and integrate activities to achieve optimal bottom-line results.
- Opportunity values (OVs) that show how much bottom-line profit will be added by overcoming active constraints.
- Performance reports that compare actual company-wide and departmental performance to any plan or set of actual results.

Readers familiar with LP technology are likely to recognize OVs as what textbooks call *shadow prices* or *marginal values*. In EO these values are referred to as opportunity values and serve as flags for opportunities to be explored, which can be done quickly by releasing the variable's constraint to see how far the profit model goes before running into other constraints.

A powerful way to motivate people to change what they are doing is with a specific, enticing financial opportunity.

Opportunity values are good for challenging and reshaping policies, traditions, and paradigms. We tend to cling to, and rationalize, what we are already doing. A powerful way to motivate people to change what they are doing is with a specific, enticing financial opportunity. Opportunity values are the numbers we need to keep moving toward BestPossible and one of a Profit Hawk's most powerful tools.

Validation and Reconciliation

One of the most important aspects of an EO system is its credibility in the eyes of the leadership team. Counterintuitive information may be entirely accurate and, because it changes decisions, can be profoundly valuable. However, if the Profit Hawk can't quickly assure his or her team that the model is accurate, leaders can be hesitant to accept the opportunities exposed, and thus waste time and profits.

The validation processes designed into the systems identify data and logic problems. Data discrepancies usually occur as a result of data-collection problems or mistakes. An erroneous extra zero on a material cost can cause major distortions in model results. LP model validation is a regular process that assures reliable decision support.

Beyond validation, periodic reconciliation of the model results to the company's financial reporting assures that the model logic is sound. Logic errors are easy to recognize because they cause either obviously unreasonable results or "can't get there from here" infeasibilities. To ensure accuracy, the model's sales and resource limits are constrained to match those of a recent accounting period, and the model's pro forma income statement is verified for acceptable variances.

Q *This all seems so complicated. Where do we start? How long will it take to see results?*

A Profit optimization is mathematically complicated, but software handles the hard parts. The best way to get started is by proclaiming BestPossible to be your destination. Once you gain team acceptance, you will find everything else about your journey to BestPossible is quite straightforward. Once the right things to do have been identified, getting them done well is not complicated.

You can expect to see positive results almost immediately. Creativity kicks in, and good things happen when people know their destination and how to get there. As quickly as you can implement your BestPossible scoreboard (see chapter 9), you can start measuring and documenting your team's climb from baseline profits.

Chapter 11

Summary and Comments

If we could write the magic phrase, or send the special message, that would enable you to achieve your BestPossible our mission would be complete. Since we haven't landed on either of those, our hope is that this book will start you and your team towards your BestPossible.

We have enormous respect for leaders and the challenges of leadership and we hope that Profit Hawks is something worthwhile for you. Obviously this book could be longer, filled with stories and first-hand accounts of success to further convince the skeptical, our editors and independent reviewers even said as much. However, we are writing for you, the movers and shakers in the business world. Out of respect for your time and intelligence we offer this concise, self-reflective style. After all, most of us learn best by doing and the sooner you start the more profits you will capture.

Near the beginning of this book, we asked if you were able to validate each of a series of statements that pertains to EO. As you become a Profit Hawk, these principles will become clear, and your job will be to help your team understand them. Are you ready to share the following principles of EO?

- The greatest opportunities for any business lie beyond the self-imposed limits that shape its paradigms.
- Once quantified, all constraints that hold your enterprise back are surmountable.
- Enterprise Optimization is more efficient, rewarding, and effective than accounting-based decision-making systems, and most importantly, it feeds your creativity.
- BestPossible gets better as we get better and as we gain resources and skills and as our team becomes more confident, creative, systematic, and enthusiastic—in other words, more effective.

Once you apply yourself as a Profit Hawk, you will be able to routinely quantify your contribution to the profit growth of the company. No other roles in an organization can provide the same level of sustained contribution—none. Moreover, as a Profit Hawk, you can stop wondering if the goals and plans you are developing are really optimal, or even viable, or whether the results were primarily a function of your leadership efforts or the market factors.

Ultimately, the EO practice as a Profit Hawk is a universally valuable discipline that will serve you in all aspects of your life and professional career.

Terms and Concepts

Enterprise Optimization

EO is a systematic process of decision-making that optimizes planning, integrating, coordinating, and executing all dimensions of enterprise activities. It is used to overcome human limitations and improve on traditional decision-support methods. Its potential is related to these universal truths:

- The decisions you and your team make directly and inevitably determine your level of success.
- All companies have never-ending, profit-sensitive decisions to make.
- Complexities of trade-offs and ripple effects obscure opportunities to earn additional bottom-line profits.

A New Game

Business management is more demanding and complex than we like to accept. The contents of this book make it clear why your full potential is not achievable without the help of optimization technologies to analyze the many complexities of a management team's decision environment.

Leading based on opportunity, recognizing the full-context implications of decisions, measuring profit gaps, motivating teams to overcome constraints, and providing ever higher levels of customer service have always been aspirational ideas. And now, thanks to EO, they are very real, necessary, and viable parts of the leadership game.

Four Modes of Enterprise Optimization

Mode 1—Creative Offense

Great tools enable great leadership. By allowing company
leaders to see clearly where
their opportunities reside, and
to prioritize the efforts through
use of all-things-considered *opportunity values*, they are
assured of best-possible plans.

	Creative	Systematic
Offense	Innovative **1**	Progressive **2**
Defense	Corrective **4**	Protective **3**

Mode 2—Systematic Offense

Fully integrated and coordinated *profit plans* assure that all aspects of operational activities are in alignment. When new
constraints appear, as they inevitably do, the systems facilitate
immediate course corrections.

Mode 3—Systematic Defense

When on protective defense, the systems are used effectively to
identify, quantify, and address profit-limiting effects of outdated policies, practices, and traditions.

Mode 4—Creative Defense

Unexpected problems, breakdowns, and crises happen. When
they do, EO is used to facilitate creative and timely solutions.

Leading a company is both an art and a science. Creative
planning is a right-brain function, while putting those plans to

work requires left-brain discipline. Company leaders and managers need to be creative and systematic to advance their levels of success.

The Five Game Pieces

Every game requires some form of equipment or playing pieces. In the game of *Enterprise Optimization*, there are five playing pieces. All pieces are necessary to play, and there are no others that can be substituted. They are your five classes of resources.

There can be no advancement without change, and there can be no change without the expenditures of resources. This means the process is really about the procurement and use of these resources, by weighing big-picture effects of all choices and making decisions for maximum advantage.

A company's five resources are these:

1. Capital
2. Procurement options
3. Sales opportunities
4. Production capabilities
5. Information

As we work to optimize our operations, we must regularly look beyond existing resources to include those we can acquire. We advance by the strengths of our resources and our skills in using them. To advance substantially, we must add to our strengths and our skills.

The Five Business Constituents

In addition to the five game pieces, every company has five basic constituents upon which they depend for survival, advancement, and lasting prosperity. In order of foundational importance they are (1) community, (2) customers, (3) suppliers, (4) employees, and (5) owners.

Field of Opportunities

Your profit gap is also your field of opportunities. By the nature of the business world, opportunities to improve enterprise performance come in many varieties, shapes, and sizes; inside the box and outside the box; within traditions and perceptions; as simple and complex; as strategic, tactical, and operational; and among procurement, production, and sales.

The more we learn about where to look for opportunities, the better prepared we will be to recognize and capture the best of them as they unfold or otherwise appear. We already know this much: all growth will reside somewhere within our fields of opportunities—somewhere between our present positions and our unique BestPossible.

The EO Scoreboard

Every company's profits reflect market and leadership factors— to ensure progress, we need to understand and monitor these two factors. EO systems are uniquely capable of filtering out market effects on bottom-line profits to provide undistorted views of true management performance—the kind of feedback we need for optimal policy and course adjustments. They produce measures independent of market forces including these indexes:

Performance Index

As market prices change, so do profits. However, market-driven price changes are not uniform among products or geographical regions. The Performance Index (PI) measures how well we have adjusted and coordinated our procurement, production, and sales activities in response to shifting market conditions to achieve our goals.

Achievement Index

The Achievement Index (AI) shows each period's profit performance as a percentage of the period's optimal target.

Creativity Index

The Creativity Index (CI) measures each month's gain or loss in the company's profit potential relative to its baseline. This shows how creative the management team is being at overcoming profit constraints and increasing its potential.

BestPossible and Beyond

BestPossible is not something to do until something better comes along. Nothing can be better.

New technologies liberate us to achieve superlative results. By putting the right technologies in the hands of trained and empowered people, Profit Hawks enables and fuels the art and science of Enterprise Optimization. A BestPossible enterprise is like a perpetual-motion machine where the company's capital is its fuel—as long as it can generate more than it consumes, it can go on forever.

In closing, here are the essential lessons we hoped to share through this book:

- Every company has an achievable BestPossible—which is only achievable if it is known.

- We are witness to the emergence of EO technologies as its necessity becomes widely recognized; those who lead in its use will enjoy lasting competitive advantages.

- Any company can become a BestPossible company simply by acknowledging it as its destination and relentlessly pursuing it.

- Profit Hawks are the masters of the bottom line. Their roles equip companies to perform as BestPossible enterprises.

- Enterprise Optimization is not one of those flavor-of-the-month initiatives that will get displaced by the next leadership innovation. The greatest rewards have always been, and will always be, the result of pursuing optimal performance.

For further information, visit us at www.profithawk.com or contact us by email at info@profithawk.com.

Enjoy your journey.

Additional Resources

EO Software Services
- Email: info@profithawk.com
- Website: www.profithawk.com

Engagement Process:
1. Ninety-minute key-personnel discovery session
2. Thirty-day opportunity analysis/modeling

Other Services
- Email: info@profithawk.com
- Keynote speaking
- EO presentations
- EO workshops/boot camps

EO Reading List (by date)
1. Krotov, Yury and Andrew Bielat. "Profit Optimization in the Steel Industry: Profit Hawk™ Application." December 2015, *Iron & Steel Technology.*
2. Bartlett, Randy. *A Practitioner's Guide to Business Analytics: Using Data Analysis Tools to Improve Your Organization's Decision-Making and Strategy.* New York: McGraw-Hill, 2013.
3. Bryan, Eugene and Andrew Bielat. *The BestPossible Enterprise: A Comprehensive Guide to Optimal Profits.* Seattle:

Aylesbury Publishing, 2013.

4. Collins, James C. and Morten T. Hansen. *Great by Choice*. Boston: Harvard Business Press, 2011.

5. Stubbs, Evan. *The Value of Business Analytics*. New York: John Wiley & Sons, 2011.

6. Cox, J. III and J. Schleier. *Theory of Constraints Handbook*. New York: McGraw-Hill Professional, 2010.

7. Davenport, Thomas H. and Jeanne G. Harris. *Competing on Analytics: The New Science of Winning*. Boston: Harvard Business School Press, 2007.

8. Eden, Y. and B. Roaz. *Approximately Right, Not Precisely Wrong: Cost Accounting, Pricing & Decision-Making*. North River Press, 2007.

9. McDonald, Mark and Tina Nunno. *Creating Enterprise Leverage: The 2007 CIO Agenda*. Stamford, CT: Gartner, Inc., 2007.

10. Pfeffer, Jeffrey and Robert I. Sutton. "Evidence-Based Management." *Harvard Business Review*, 2006.

11. Ranadive, Vivek. *The Power to Predict: How Real-Time Businesses Anticipate Customer Needs, Create Opportunities, and Beat the Competition*. New York: McGraw-Hill, 2006.

12. Davenport, Thomas H. and Jeanne G. Harris. "Automated Decision-Making Comes of Age." MIT *Sloan Management Review*, 2005.

13. Caspari, J. A. and P. Caspari. Management Dynamics: Merging Constraints Accounting to Drive Improvement. New York: Wiley, 2004.

14. Lewis, Michael. *Moneyball: The Art of Winning an Unfair Game*. New York: W.W. Norton & Co., 2004.

15. Bryan, Eugene. *BestPossible Profits: Guidebook for Forest Products Companies*. Madison, WI: Forest Products Society, 2003.

16. Zabin, Jeffrey and Gresh, Brebach. *Precision Marketing.* New York: John Wiley, 2004.
17. Bonabeau, Eric. "Don't Trust Your Gut." *Harvard Business Review*, 2003.
18. Bryan, Eugene. *The BestPossible Sawmill: Guidebook for the High-Tech Journey Ahead.* San Francisco: Miller Freeman Books, 1996.
19. Goldratt, E. M. and J. Cox. *The Goal: A Process of Ongoing Improvement.* New York: North River Press, 1986.

Acknowledgments

I want to thank my dad, Chester Bielat, USMC–WWII, for instilling in me that there is a best way to do anything, from digging a ditch to running a company. Thank you to my trusting and supportive clients, who have made my career rich and exciting. I could not be where I am without the great people I have worked with and am working with today.

A special thanks to Dan Zeamer for introducing me to Gene Bryan and his concepts of BestPossible®, enabling me to fully realize my mission and share it with my clients and readers. Finally, I can't thank Gene, Elaine, and Linda Bryan enough for the unfettered access to, and collaboration with, the Bryan family.

Andrew Bielat

First and foremost, I thank my ever-loving wife, Elaine, for her many supportive roles in my life, career, and writings. Over almost five decades, I have enjoyed working with hundreds of enthusiastic clients. I thank them all for their innovative applications of our concepts and tools. Their progressive leadership, dedication, creativity, and field-tested suggestions have greatly contributed to the art and science of Enterprise Optimization.

I am pleased to acknowledge and thank Andrew Bielat for joining me in my mission to spread the word and as a leading advocate for Enterprise Optimization. I owe special thanks to Mike Golovnykh, CTO, Profit Hawk, for his keen mind and eye in critiquing our work and enabling it through his software development and applications.

Eugene Bryan

About the Authors

Andrew C. Bielat

Without realizing it, Andrew has been consistently focusing his life and career choices along the path leading to his BestPossible.

He was adopted into a working-class family in the early 1960s and learned from his loving, hardworking parents to do the best he could at whatever he did. He started his first company at the age of twelve and never stopped. Andrew put himself through college and earned a bachelor of science degree in mechanical engineering with honors from the University of Illinois, Urbana-Champaign.

Andrew's early professional career was a fast track to senior leadership positions within the consumer food, nuclear power, and steel industries. He realized his entrepreneurial ambitions when, in 1997, he founded Pilot Advisors. As an executive coach and performance advisor, he combined his leadership expertise and engineering discipline to build a thriving firm. He and his team have served a large, diverse list of clients, including *Fortune* 100 companies, family-owned businesses, the Department of Defense, and the Department of Energy. He has personally worked with over seventy-five companies, coached dozens of executives, presented to thousands, and trained thousands more.

Andrew founded Profit Hawk, LLC, to serve what he says is "the obvious and pressing need for fact-based decision-making tools and support." Profit Hawk is a cloud-based, award-winning, patents-pending Enterprise Optimization system.

Andrew has been a featured speaker on television—namely, *21st Century Business* aired on Fox Business News and on CNBC—and on radio—*Talk Business 360*, heard on the major airlines. He is a keynote speaker and presenter at leadership summits such Managing Automation's Progressive Leadership Summit.

Eugene L. Bryan, Ph.D.

Gene is best known for his groundbreaking work and publications in the field of computer-based Enterprise Optimization—a technology he pioneered and refined over many years as he helped hundreds of companies go for best-possible performance. Gene now works through his company, BestPossible Solutions, Inc., as a consultant and author while continuing to advance, promote, and apply his advanced management concepts and supportive technologies.

Gene earned a bachelor of science degree from the University of Idaho, two masters of science degrees from the University of California, Berkeley, and a PhD from the University of Michigan.

Before BestPossible Solutions, he founded and served as president and CEO of Decision Dynamics, Inc., of Lake Oswego, Oregon, where for thirty years his company worked throughout the United States and internationally serving firms ranging from family-owned operations to *Fortune* 500 corporations.

In 2012, Gene joined forces with Andrew Bielat and Profit Hawk, LLC, to stay active in helping private-sector enterprises discover and enjoy the many benefits of computer-based Enterprise Optimization.

32503873R00068

Made in the USA
Middletown, DE
07 June 2016